Parallel Worlds

LINDA R. MARTIN

PAGE PUBLISHING, INC.
Conneaut Lake, PA

First originally published by Page Publishing 2021

ISBN 978-1-6624-4578-1 (pbk)
ISBN 978-1-6624-4579-8 (digital)

Printed in the United States of America

To every free-spirited person in the world with a dream who loves life.

To all the people who went through the hardship of socialism. God got us through it.

To my family.

To my grandparents, who put up with my rebel ways, trying to understand my fight against oppression and misery. I was searching for the light out of socialism.

To my daughter, a free-spirited, beautiful person. The sky is the limit for you, baby, and keep on dreaming.

To my best friend Leeland, who is working on his dreams right now with LEGOs, but keep on dreaming, buddy. I love you.

To the people who made their way out of the socialism prison of Romania, illegally crossing the borders, risking their lives and their families' lives, trying to find a better place to live, and trying to reach free countries in this world. Thank God there are free countries in this world that respect the value of life and appreciate the human being.

To the woman with the little baby that stood behind me in the milk line in the middle of the very cold night. You are one of my heroes, trying to protect life, the life of the baby. God bless us all.

All the people that I dedicate this book to are very important to me. I would like to dedicate this book to my chemistry teacher also. Yes! Thank you for uncovering the real you and how many like you believed in a humanity-degrading system, a system of fear, a system of hunger, lies, manipulation, and a futureless system, which others like you believed. You and the others increased my love of life and freedom many times over. Thank you, and God bless.

—Cristian

To every child who has ever gone to bed hungry. Food not only supplies the nutrients children need to grow and flourish but also creates a sense of security and stability. Food is what makes a holiday special. It helps in making a house a home. To these children, I pledge any proceeds on this book to assist in feeding you and your families. You deserve to grow and flourish. Just like me, so many others do care.

To God as He made it possible for me to never understand the conditions these children endure.

To my grandmother, who made certain I felt secure and knew the meaning of love and family.

—Linda

PROLOGUE

He told me he remembers being born. No one has ever said that to me before. I also remember the light of birth but never told a living soul. I can still see that light so vividly that I could draw it but never have. I think he felt the same. The connection was immediate and almost tangible. His honesty was refreshing, but with that honesty came a story I never expected to hear.

Growing up in the 1970s, we all knew Europe as beautiful, historic, and peaceful. The story I heard was exactly the opposite. As a US citizen, I now realize just how much I took for granted, how much I didn't know, how two lives are lived in parallel halfway across the world at the same time but so differently, and how much history is so relevant to the world as we know and live today.

CHAPTER 1

Parallel Worlds

Traveling to West Virginia in the summer of 2020 to visit a family of close friends, I expected to be surrounded by a group of sweet, southern voices and incredible hospitality. I went to visit a family I had known for thirty-five years that lived in a small town in very close proximity to one another. They loved children and gatherings. They loved company and sharing their home. Like all good southern folks, they were food pushers, huggers, and storytellers, and I needed to be with good people at this time in my life. I had just ended a thirty-five-year marriage and lived alone for the very first time in my entire life. There were times when friends feel and behave more like family than those whose blood runs through your veins. This is the reason I went to visit. What I didn't expect was Cristian. He was part of the family by marriage and divorce that I had never met before. He was certainly the anomaly in the small town of Elkins. Cristian had a strong European accent that could melt through cold butter and all the swagger of a man confident with his presence—sexy, charming, strong, and handsome. He also cursed like a sailor and smoked like a chimney, much like me when I'm not around my white-collar colleagues.

His voice immediately woke something up in me that had been buried deep for many years. The flirting was exhilarating. The attention was intoxicating. Exiting a toxic marriage after thirty-five years,

I had felt human, but not feminine, not sensual in any way, shape, or form. I had given up on that a long time ago. I felt like I was a teenager again, and I loved that feeling. I finally asked Cristian for a bedtime story, thinking I was going to get a sensual and erotic series of words spoken in that incredibly sexy European accent. When he started telling his story, I knew immediately that is not what I was going to hear.

He started telling me about his life growing up in the same 1970s era as I did but from halfway around the world in Romania, a country I knew nothing about. When I think of all the history classes throughout my education here in the United States, not once do I remember reading anything about the world he lived and told me about through a series of bedtime stories. What I thought was going to be a simple, sexual encounter turned into a life-altering realization of how everything I knew about growing up in the United States for the past fifty years was taken for granted and unappreciated. His story made me understand how incredibly lucky and privileged I was to be born and raised in the United States of America.

Cristian started telling me his story about growing up in Romania in the early 1970s as a very young boy. He remembers being two years old, which I found incredible. Not many people have clear memories of themselves at that young age or at least none of the people I talk to. It started sweet and very detailed, and as he told the story, I found myself already starting to compare my memories at those same ages nearly five thousand miles away, halfway around the world in the United States of America. He remembers being a happy and carefree two-year-old child who would run through his grandparents' apartment in Deva, Romania, a city in central Romania on the left bank of the Mures River. As he spoke of such a young memory, I too remember being very young, close to two years old, trying to form words that sounded like babbling. I remember my father couldn't understand what I was trying to tell him and being very frustrated with him because he was not comprehending the story I was telling.

Cristian recalled his third birthday more vividly. His grandma bought him a robe with locomotives on it because she knew he had an infatuation with trains. He saw trains on black-and-white television and was in awe of the sheer power of these trains carrying freight and people. The robe was warm and beautiful, but what it represented was bigger than life and so powerful. He loved it. I understand at this point that his grandparents raised him, but as I asked about his parents, he evades the answers, so I didn't push on what must be a sensitive subject. I remember the day I turned three as well, opening the front door of my grandma's house and screaming to the entire neighborhood, "I'm three! I'm three!" I didn't care about presents or cake—just wanted the entire world to know I turned three. My grandmother was not happy with my behavior and scurried to grab me from the front door to end my campaign. My parents had an incredibly unhealthy relationship, and by the time I turned three, my father had left us, and my mother took us to her mother's house to live. Like Cristian, I felt happy and safe with my grandparents. Our young childhoods seem so similar, and I don't think I ever had a conversation with someone who remembered their third birthday before him as I did.

When Cristian told me about his fourth birthday in February 1974, I completely related to this story when most people would be appalled. His uncle and aunt came to visit him at his grandparents' home. The uncle was a doctor and also Cristian's godfather. He brought the young boy a very unusual present, a box of wild cherry liqueur-filled chocolate eggs. Cristian remembered eating one and very much enjoying it. He loved the flavor but also how it made him feel. He then began drinking the liqueur from all the others. He remembered this amazing feeling of being happy and light-headed, laughing and attempting to walk around the apartment. The next thing he remembered was the four elders calling his name, looking for him because he had passed out on the floor behind the couch, but he couldn't answer them to tell his whereabouts. Of course, when they found him, his grandma worried that he was drunk and may not be well, but the uncle, a doctor, assured her he would be fine. Cristian joked this was his first "party hearty" birthday, and I smiled. Both of my grandparents were European descendants, so we also received alcohol as children. On special occasions, there was a carafe of wine for adults and one for children, watered-down, that made us sleep very well on those nights. We also drank from grandpa's beer cans when he pretended not to watch with a huge smile on his face. Alcohol was not a big deal or forbidden for children in 1974, so this story was very relatable to me.

Cristian's grandfather worked for the Romanian government, and he never realized what a taxing position that was or the nature of what he was doing. Of course, he found out later in life while his grandfather worked for the government, he was assigned to verify the financial aspects of the mining industry in Romania. The man worked six or seven days a week, every single week of the year, but when he had a Sunday off, he would take Cristian to the train station in the spring and summer because he knew of the young boy's infatuation with locomotives. Cristian loved and respected the power of trains and adored his grandfather for taking him to the station to see them up close and in real life. Our worlds still seemed very similar. My mother worked so many hours that my grandparents were my caretaker as well. My grandmother did not work, and my grandfather would generally work five days a week and the occasional Saturday.

Other Sundays, Cristian's grandma would take him to church. One particular Sunday, Cristian remembered his grandmother taking him to the train station after church, probably knowing his grandfather would not be able to. I could hear the smile in his voice as he told the story of the smaller steam engine stopping right in front of him that day by the first track. It was maneuvering on the track, building cars to create the freight train. I visualized the smile on a young boy's face lighting up the train station because the train had actually stopped right in front of him, and he could see the conductor who actually motioned him to climb aboard. Of course, his grandmother was hesitant because Cristian would get his church clothes dirty on that train, and she was always trying to keep him clean and presentable. She gave in to his excitement and allowed him to join the conductor, helping the young child up the stairs. Once in the engine, he was too small to see out the window of the train but saw all the levers and controls. The conductor told Cristian to pull the lever, and when he pulled it back, the train actually moved backward. He described this as the first dream come true—being on that train and having been able to move that train with so much weight. He remembered skipping all the way home from the train station in his church clothes, now soiled. My first dream come true also occurred in 1974 when my father sent money to his mother to buy me a Barbie Dreamhouse for my birthday. I remember it seemed to be taller than me, although I'm sure it was not. There were multiple rooms and stories, and all I could think about was the fun I was going to have to play with my best friend, who lived two doors away.

As Cristian remembered his grandparents, he talked about how attached he was to them because they were his caretakers and providers. They supplied all the basic necessities like shelter, bed, heat, water, and food, but there was also a lot of love in the house. They went as a family to the market every weekend to buy groceries for the week. In 1974, there was no shortage of food in Romania. The grocery stores were full of milk, meat, cheese, produce, bread, and everything a child would want to eat. Cristian remembered he was always confused about why the Swiss cheese had holes in it and would ask his grandparents, "Who ate those holes in the cheese?" His grandparents would laugh and play along with the child to make the shopping trip fun. I'm sure there were children in the United States that went grocery shopping with their family, but I did not. Food was always in the refrigerator, and I had no idea how it got there. There was always a pot of tea on the stove, a cake in the cake dish, and candy in Grandpa's pocket. My grandparents were very special to me as well and for the same reasons as Cristian. Not only did they supply the necessities, but there was so much love. Throughout my entire life, they were the two people I adored more than any other human being. The smell of my grandparent's home is my favorite scent— Italian gravy, coffee, air-dried linens, and cigarette smoke. That may not sound appealing to many people, but it smells like heaven to me.

In 1977, Cristian's grandpa was sent to the United States for two weeks to establish contacts with bigger companies making dump trucks and excavators to carry coal and iron ore. He remembered the day his grandpa left for the train station and asking his grandfather to go to New York and get himself on TV so that he knows his grandpa is all right. Previously, they had watched a series on television about a New York sheriff we all know as McCloud, and to a young child, it seemed like a real place to visit. His grandpa knew the sheriff as a fictional character but told Cristian he would try to find McCloud and be on television. After his grandfather left for the United States, there was an earthquake in Romania and not just an earthquake but it was the second largest, most powerful of the twentieth century in Romania with a magnitude of 7.2. It was devastating to the country and to this small child. Cristian remembered being so worried about his grandfather's well-being until he arrived home. His grandpa did arrive safely shortly after. We also had an earthquake in the city I lived in that year. Although not near the magnitude, it still worried me enough to try to hold up the walls in the house after waking up in the middle of the night yelling to grandma, "Earthquake!" The first time you experience something as grand as an earthquake, you just never forget, and being a child made it even more terrifying.

That same year, Cristian was made pioneer by the communist regime when he was in second grade. This means, he wore a red tie around his neck and had to swear allegiance to the communist system. He was sworn in the city park with his entire class led by his teacher. The ceremony included each child, male and female, to touch the flag with their right hand and swear allegiance to the communist system. As Cristian told this story, I thought to myself how it didn't seem much different than me pledging allegiance to the United States of America every morning at 8:00 a.m. in school while holding my right hand on my heart and facing the American flag. A child will recite whatever you tell them to say at this age. Pledging allegiance to your country was normal—patriotic, bonding. There were no choices in these matters. As a child, you simply learned and obeyed. You didn't question your government, and you did not overhear your parents questioning these rituals either. Children were taught to respect the country, the flag, and what it represented, whether that's in the United States or Romania.

Life in the United States and Romania did not seem very different at this point. As Cristian spoke about his memories, it was really nice thinking about mine, times I hadn't conjured up in my head for a long time. It actually helped me to remember the good in life—the times filled with genuine love.

CHAPTER 2

The Fork in the Road

In 1977, Jimmy Carter became president of the United States. I was very young, but I remember grown-ups wondering how a peanut farmer from Georgia became the president of the United States. Looking back at their ignorance of this man, it was obvious he had a solid agenda. He was the dark horse in the 1976 election and was not well known outside his home state of Georgia. He opposed racial segregation and supported the civil rights movement. On his second day in office, he pardoned all Vietnam War draft evaders. During his term, the Department of Energy and the Department of Education were established. It was obvious Jimmy Carter loved this country and the citizens who lived here. He embraced diversity, domestic equality, optimism, and change.

In the fall of 1977, Nicolae Ceausescu was the president of Romania and the communist party. He had been the president since 1974 and had made some very ambitious investments trying to build oil refineries in Romania during the 1970's energy crisis. He borrowed heavily from Western banks and, when those loans came due, did not have the oil refineries up and running to make payments due to poor planning and the 1977 earthquake that destroyed much of Bucharest.

President Ceausescu was televised in the fall of 1977 to speak about the wasting of so much food by the Romanian people and that he was concerned for their welfare. He announced that he would reduce the quantity of food but make the quality of the food better. He assured the Romanian people that there would still be enough food for everyone to eat and not to be concerned. Not only did Cristian watch this live on television, but it was also discussed in school. Schools were used as the media to promote socialism and communism to young children. In fact, the schools would teach these young children that socialism was better than communism and that they should be very happy living in a socialist country. Although hearing about a reduction in food on television and in school, he was not worried at that time because he was repeatedly told there would still be enough food. He did tell me, however, the news was filed in the back of his head as something that stuck, something he would never forget. Although we heard several times a day as a child throughout the 1970s of an energy crisis, not enough fuel, families having to take turns at the gas pumps, it did not worry me as a child because my life was not impacted in any way, shape or form. My grandfather and mother both seemed to have gas in the car to get to work. Even being lower-middle class, we always had food on the table.

In 1979, another announcement was made by President Ceausescu stating some changes would need to be made in the lifestyle of the Romanian people, but it would all be for the best. Cristian remembered that year, the food really started to change. It was not the same quality. Cheese started to disappear, and what was left was certainly not the same as it had been prior. As other food items started to disappear off the market, Cristian became worried and, again, filed this in his memory. I could not comprehend a shortage of food. It didn't make sense to me. How and why could a president of any country purposely create a food shortage?

In 1980, a lot of other food items started disappearing off the store shelves as soon as it was stocked, so lines started to form at the markets. Romanian citizens would start lining up the night before in an attempt to get necessities. One Saturday, his grandpa took him grocery shopping, as they always did, but there were many more people in the store. When he asked his grandpa why there are so many people, his grandpa asked him to be quiet. They left the store without food for the first time. There were people reaching over the counter for any food that was left—not so much a fight as a battle. Cristian, an inquisitive and hungry child, asked his grandpa why there was no food and what they would do. As they left the store, his grandpa had a very worried look on his face. Obviously, a look that Cristian remembers to this day. His grandpa simply took him home, which made Cristian mad at his grandpa until he saw the very serious look on his grandpa's face—the look that told him, "This is bad"— the look that made him worry this is the beginning of a time where there would be suffering. I can't even fathom what must have been a horrible memory for him. Sure we all know what a grocery store looks like when the weather forecast is heavy snow or a hurricane, but this was not the case here. There was literally no food at the grocery store, and no one understood why at this time. He remembered going to school, and many of the children were no longer bringing food. Cristian couldn't get a handle on what was going on. When I asked him what he ate on a daily basis as a ten-year-old child, he told me lunch was a couple of slices of bread with honey or occasionally cured bacon (although not very often), a very watery soup, but it was hot. If his grandma got chicken, she was able to add it. Then at bedtime, so that he could sleep, hot tea with honey or a couple of crackers were served to give him calories. Bread was rationalized but was still available. The bread was not the same as he remembered. It was whole grain and brown. This was enough to get his stomach full so he could sleep.

This story punched my stomach and sank my heart. It was now filed in the back of my mind, and I couldn't unhear it. There was no way to relate or rationalize it. I had to research why this president would create a food shortage for his own people. I understood how he had the power in a socialist country but needed to know why. What I found out is that the Romanian government was selling its crops to other countries to pay off debt and leaving the Romanian people with only the third-grade food produced that could not be sold and certainly not enough of it. Communism, socialist dictatorship made it possible for this to occur without question. While the president of the United States was fighting for the rights and education of the citizens, this evil dictator was ordering Romanian citizens to eat less than 1,200 calories per day, eventually down to 800 calories. All citizens were mandated regardless of age, gender, or health.

Eventually, President Ceausescu called for energy savings. In that same year, the power went out one night in the middle of the night unannounced. The citizens of Romania were not warned. His grandma woke up worried, and that woke up Cristian and his grandpa. He remembered the power coming back on at 6:00 a.m. The power would now start to go out in the evenings and start coming back on in the mornings on a regular basis. Next, the hot water was also rationalized. In some apartments, it was only turned on one day a week. This young boy couldn't understand why hot water would be rationalized and received only a couple of hours daily, sometimes in the morning and sometimes at night. It was very difficult to get ready for school and wash up with ice-cold water coming from the faucets. This all became the normal day after day, week after week, month after month, and year after year. Little to no food or milk, daily power outages, and only a couple of days with hot water.

As a ten-year-old in the United States, we had all the necessities, not always an abundance of money, but we never worried about food, electricity, or hot water. We worried about memorizing all the words for the school recitals, getting permission slips signed for field trips, which boy liked which girl, and picking our outfits for school the next day—normal childhood concerns.

When school started in September 1980 in Romania, the teacher told the class of ten-year-old children that they had to do patriotic work every Sunday in the city and in the fields. She told them there was much that needed to be done; they would be cleaning the city—all free labor from ten-year-old children on their only day off from school. Cristian wondered how a ten-year-old would work, for free, eight to ten hours a day on the weekend and still be able to complete schoolwork. School in Romania was Monday through Saturday, which meant the only day off on Sunday would be dedicated to this patriotic work. There would not be any breaks. There were no labor laws, no child-protection agencies. Parents were forbidden to refuse the children from going. These children would take a bus to the city and work for free every Sunday.

In the late fall, Cristian's grandma bought a small radio from a Polish tourist, and Cristian could hear his grandma listening to the radio after she put him to bed. His grandparents would listen to the news, and Cristian wondered what was going on. The children at school would also talk about their parents listening to these radios, which he later found out were illegal radio that aired stations from West Germany in Berlin called Free Europe and Voice of America. Both stations were sponsored by the United States government. Although the young children didn't understand at this time, there was criticism of the communist regime and the inhumane treatment of the citizens of Romania. These radio stations still exist today and can be heard in online versions.

Of course, since the children were able to gain access to these radios, Cristian started listening when he could but not to the news. He listened to music—music that he had been previously banned from hearing. The children of Romania had never heard music from America, France, or Germany. Cristian loved it. There were two music radio segments called By Request and Metronome. He would take the radio to the place in the apartment where the signal was the best, and that was his grandma's room. He would climb up on the radiator heater on Saturday and Sunday and listen to the music. These stations were sponsored by the United States government, so he would listen to Michael Jackson, Queen, Bob Seager. He loved the music, the instruments, the beat. Music became a passion and what appeared to be an escape from the harsh world he lived in. Listening to these radio stations, Cristian started dreaming with his eyes open about what it would be like to grow up in another country like America, Germany, France, Italy—countries where he heard citizens had the basic necessities in life. The power does not go out daily in those countries. They have hot water. There is no shortage of food. They have the freedom to travel, visit where they want, and enjoy life. "Why do they have cheese and bologna and chocolate and bananas?" Cristian explained that he kept going back to food because he remembered being a young child when the stores were full of food, and now there was none. He hoped one day to see cheese again with holes in it and wonder how the holes got in the cheese.

By the time it was 1980 in the United States, we had already been heavily exposed to the Beatles, Rolling Stones, Elton John, David Bowie, and other genres like disco, and rap had just started. I loved music too—had to know every word to every song and buy every number one album on the charts. Cristian and I would debate the best decade of music forever. He started listening in the 1980s, so that's what he's more passionate about. My grandmother played 1950s music. My mother played 1960s music. Fact is, I am sure I was conceived to Mel Carter singing "Hold Me, Thrill Me, Kiss Me," but that's just me thinking. I remember it, not because my mother ever told me this was true, nor have I ever asked. I love it all, but my favorite is the seventies because that's when I started to form my own interest in music. Fact is, most of my playlist today is from that era. It's so hard to understand someone having to actually sneak to listen to music illegally. It was everywhere in America—cars, homes, stores, movies, television, schools. We were encouraged to listen and sing.

In the winter of 1980 in Romania, right before Christmas break, the power went out, and it was very cold outside, and Cristian could see his breath in his bedroom. He was dressed in several layers of clothes, lying beside glass bottles filled with hot water so he could sleep. Life was getting harder every day. Television and schools would promote how good this president was and how much he was providing for the people. The stories would encourage citizens to work harder. Citizens actually believed it. Schools were no exception. There were not heated, and although it was very cold in school, children were not allowed to leave their coats on. This was to ensure their uniforms were displayed at all times, even though that meant they were cold. In the United States, if the heater was not working at a school, there would be no classes. Children were not expected to be where there was no heat.

In 1980, Cristian's brother was born into this hardship. The child would not know what it was like to buy food in a store or to have heat and hot water every day. Cristian's mom had to get in touch with the Red Cross to get powdered milk for the bottles for his brother. Regular milk could not be found in the stores. Lines would form daily at nine o'clock in the evening for the following day, and at least one hundred people would wait in those lines until the next morning. I know it was necessary for his mother to work and to think breast pumps were not available to Romanian citizens. They didn't have the necessities like food and electricity, so nonessentials were probably very difficult to obtain.

The same year, the school staff announced that the children must bring food to school to prove children ate. There had been stories circulating that children were starving, so the request for food in schools was a cover-up to prove they were eating. He remembered maybe 30 percent of the children brought a slice of bread wrapped in a napkin while the rest brought nothing. When the parents of the children were questioned as to why these children did not bring food as ordered, the parents tried to explain to teachers that they work because they need money and then have to try to wait in line for food that isn't at the store when they go. Cristian was given the ultimatum by his grandma to either take an apple to school and have a modest dinner or drink water at school and eat a bigger dinner. I think to myself, what an incredibly hard thing to ask of a child as his caretaker. Then I think of what a difficult decision that had to be for a small boy.

In 1980, the United States elected a famous movie star, Ronald Reagan, as its president. The winter Olympics were proudly hosted in Lake Placid, New York. An American citizen freely created Mothers Against Drunk Driving (MADD), Pac Man is the best-selling arcade game, CNN is created and received famously, and our hometown Philadelphia Phillies won their first World Series. The biggest story of this year in the United States was the Iran Hostage Crisis. We all saw it on the news daily, talked about it at home and in school, and it became a very political event during the election. There was also poverty in the United States but not in every home and certainly not because our government was selling our food and shutting off electricity at will.

In 1981 and 1982, word spread that other parts of Romania were even worse than the conditions in Deva. At the end of the 1981–1982 school year, the teacher had given all the students an assignment to collect four pounds of cranberries per student. In the summer of 1982, Cristian was waiting in a very long food line of over three hundred people with his grandparents. A man in his midforties came walking by very slowly, speaking very loudly, and he took a spot right in front of the family. He pushed Cristian's grandparents as he cut in line, which infuriated him, along with the need to ensure they got the food they went after that day. When Cristian saw this, he immediately pushed the grown man down, where he landed on empty food crates. As the man tried to stand, Cristian pushed him down again harder while others in line were trying to warn him that this man was a high-ranking communist party member. The man screamed for someone to call the police. He told Cristian and his grandparents that they did not know who he is messing with and that he would have them all arrested. Cristian and his grandparents ran off and hid themselves in another line at another market, so when the police drove by looking for them five minutes later, they blended with the other citizens and were not apprehended.

On the first day of school in September 1982, the teacher gave each student an assignment to bring five pounds of snails to school. They only had one day off from school to find the snails. The snails would be used to make pâté. There was no liver to make the pâté, so snails were boiled to make a very watery pâté.

The electricity and district heating were often stopped in order to save energy, leading to unbearable winters. Availability of hot water was also restricted to one day per week in most apartments. Unannounced power cuts affected even hospitals' regular functioning: for instance, in the winter of 1983, dozens of babies in neonatal intensive care units died due to the power cuts to the incubators. Street lighting was often turned off and generally reduced to a bare minimum.

During this time, there were manifestations in the middle of the town square. Students were brainwashed and forced to make signs condemning the United States of America for creating NATO and threatening socialism. The United States was the "bad guy," and the students wanted peace, not war. These students were being taught to hate the United States.

In 1983, Cristian recalled his chemistry teacher being very tough. His teacher was a communist party member and very tough. She was nasty to students and other teachers. He told me that she had to score brownie points and kiss ass to the party. She believed to the core in the communist system, and the students needed to follow that system to the letter of the law and made his life a living hell. The teacher also had a nephew in the same class. There was a turn of events when the teacher assigned the class to create crystals. Cristian didn't know anything about creating crystals but knew a family friend who had an engineering degree in chemistry. She provided Cristian with seven or eight crystals in many colors in really nice glass containers, and he turned them in to the teacher as his assignment. None of the other students turned in any crystals, so Cristian hoped this would turn this teacher's attitude toward him around. It seemed to work as her demeanor changed. The teacher asked him who made the crystals, and he was honest with her. The teacher then asked Cristian for a report on how the crystals were made. He asked her if he completed that assignment, she would give him an "A," and she told him that she would. He then went back to the family friend who helped him create this report. Cristian said, after he turned in the report, he sensed the teacher changed, possibly trying to understand the family friend who was helping Cristian was not doing what she did for the communist party but was an intelligent woman who solely worked because it was her job. Members of the communist party did not understand how smart people worked independently from the party. The chemistry teacher eventually brought her own nephew into the picture to get credit for this report. Cristian told me the nephew was on his back like a bed monkey, getting credit for the report. Cristian and the nephew went to the regionals to present the report, and the nephew received a better grade than Cristian. Cristian couldn't understand how the nephew, who was not intelligent and had terrible handwriting, could score better than him. Cristian was angry and asked the teacher for the crystals back. She refused to give them back, telling him the crystals now belong to the party. Cristian confronted the teacher, asking her why she lied and manipulated the situation, asking her why he did not get the grade she promised and why she took credit for the crystals. She told him not to talk like that and be quiet. Cristian then realized the party members were just a bunch of liars, reaping the benefit from other people, taking credit for themselves, and stealing to present offerings to the communist party. This teacher had influence with all the high schools and would make sure Cristian had a living hell the first two years of high school.

The Gulag was a system of forced labor camps in Russia established by Joseph Stalin's long reign as dictator of the Soviet Union through the early to mid-1900s. Cristian knew the Gulag to be a work prison for those who did not believe in communism. He knew the prisons were often in regions with extreme weather conditions like Siberia and that these people were forced to do very heavy labor such as gold mining, road building, lumbering, and construction. He did not know this sort of thing also happened in Romania. This type of imprisonment for young adults also began in 1949 in the city of Pitesti, Romania. It was called the Pitesti Phenomenon. Young people who did not believe in the communist party or practiced Christianity were locked up and violently tortured in prisons in an attempt to reeducate and erase their memory of their political and religious convictions. Although this prison was eventually closed, the philosophy is why the teacher had no understanding of an educated woman working for anything other than the communist party.

That year, as Cristian continued listening to the illegal radio station Free Europe, he started listening to the news as well as music. There was a story about the Romanian communist party having a children's prison between 1948 and 1952 in Targsor, Prahova. There were eight hundred children imprisoned, and the youngest child was ten years old. These children openly opposed the regime and were prisoned because they were extremely intelligent, and the communist party feared the children would grow up and be intellectuals. They feared these children would bring to light the conditions in Romania and how the communist regime is wrong by bringing inhumane conditions to their people. They went through reeducation, lectured by members of the communist party, and if not compliant, they would be beaten, starved, and subject to inhumane living conditions. Many did not survive. This was never talked about in Romania, and this was the first he heard of it.

This all continued through 1984 when Cristian was fourteen, although television stations were still promoting the good health of the country. By now, he had lived in these conditions for years. He knew what it was like before and despised what it was like now. He was always dreaming of leaving Romania to live somewhere he could be free from this life. Right before the holidays, all students of this age must be sworn in the Young Communists Organization and swear their allegiance. The purpose of this organization was to cultivate young people into the communist party, prepping them to become members. The auditorium was used only for the purpose of social-ist and communist festivities, which were the only festivities there were. This included singing songs about how great and wonderful the president is. The auditorium held about 1,200 people, includ-ing the students, parents, teachers, and members of the communist party. Each child, in alphabetical order, would be asked to swear their allegiance to the Young Communist Organization. Cristian's name started with the letter "V," so he was one of the last to be sworn in. This was a young man who knew what the country looked like when he was very young, prosperous, thriving—and then those years of fil-ing away things in his brain and the degradation that had taken place since 1977. Years of resentment had built up. He did not support socialism or communism. He dreamed of living in democracy.

As Cristian was asked if he swore the allegiance to the Young Communist Organization, he said, "No," loud, strong, and direct "no." The entire room was quiet, and I quote Cristian saying, "So quiet, you could hear two bacteria making love." He was asked again if he swears allegiance, and again, he told them, "No." The commu-nist leaders did not know what to say because this was not a choice. Yes was the only answer. To avoid a scene or attention to Cristian, they quickly went to the next child, leaving all dumbfounded. He had been fed up with the lies, fed up with not receiving the basics of life. Every day was more miserable than the day before. His happiest moments were lying in bed, not sleeping, just lying there with his pillow, where he did not have to see the misery around him. Mornings would make him nauseous. Although he had never been to prison, he said it felt like he was going to prison each morning, having to function as a human being in this socialism. Television and newspapers were a socialist propaganda dispenser because people actually believed in this system, and the schools brainwashed his peers to answer "yes." Cristian did not, and he could not lie to himself any longer.

On the walk home, his grandpa and mother asked him why he answered "no" and asked why he couldn't just swallow it and say "yes." They were worried about what these people would do to him because he told them no. Cristian told his grandpa and mother that he just could not pledge to the Young Communist Organization. He couldn't say he "agreed with the president" and "loved the president" because he hated him, and he hated what was going on in Romania. Children stopped playing with him and started to avoid him that year, and although he never was told why, he always assumed it was because he did not pledge his allegiance to communism, and their parents must have told them to stay away from Cristian. He also knew that his grandpa did not believe in socialism or communism but did not have a choice as this was directly related to his job. To be a communist party member, you either had to know somebody, be an exceptional worker who produced results, or work for a company where all other employees were members.

In 1984, Cristian's grandfather began to worry about the antics of his grandson and told him the story of two uncles who did prison time in Romania. The two high school students were outside, talking one evening about what they were going to do after high school. A young child approached the two teens and asked what they were talking about. The two dismissed the young boy, telling him to go away and what they were discussing was none of his business. The young boy went home and told his parents the two were plotting to withdraw from the communist regime. The police came and arrested the teens at 3:00 a.m. These boys were seventeen and eighteen years old, high school students. They were taken to a prison called White Gate, another facility to reeducate young people on their political views. The prison was in eastern Romania between the Black Sea and the Danube River. No one heard from these children for five years until Cristian's grandfather contacted the Red Cross to find out their status. He found out they had been sick but survived. Cristian told me that the location of the prison was windy all the time, and the winters there were very harsh. Not many people lived in that location as they couldn't survive. The boys grew to men as they were retained for eight to ten years. Trying to build your life again in the communist regime was nearly impossible after spending time in prison, so they had a very hard life once released. Cristian understood the message his grandfather was trying to relay but told his self that he was not going to prison; however, he knew he would suffer due to his actions. —

By 1984, the United States was halfway through the first Ronald Reagan term as president with an attempted assignation in 1981. He was leading the country to peace with strength abroad. Families were starting to prosper. The concept of the International Space Station was announced. Los Angeles, California, hosted the Summer Olympics. Bruce Springsteen released "Born in the USA." The first minivan rolled off the assembly line. AIDS was discovered. Crack cocaine was introduced. I do not remember any news or education about what was occurring in Romania.

CHAPTER 3

Dreaming with My Eyes Open

Romanian high schools were a bit different from those in the United States. There were specialty schools for mining, energy, construction, chemistry, and sports. Cristian signed up for the energy high school near his home in Deva. His first two years of high school were very rough. The teachers and faculty made it very hard for him, and he was certain the chemistry teacher, who had been in the communist party, had influenced this. She knew Cristian as the young man who would not pledge his allegiance to the Young Communist Party and also questioned her integrity when she took his project and made it her own offering.

In tenth grade, Cristian decided to apply for the mining high school and tested very well. This proved to be a bit better, but then in the first part of eleventh, his teacher asked him why he refused in eighth grade to take the pledge of the Young Communist Organization. She knew his history. The teacher was a nice person and was genuinely concerned for Cristian. He told her that he did not believe in the communist system and could not make the pledge. She advised Cristian that even though he feels that way, he lives in that system and will continue to live his life in this system, get a job, be a citizen. She was trying to help him come to the realization that he needed to be more receptive to socialism and communism to have an easier life. He summed it up by saying, "You can't piss in the wind and not get your shoes dirty." His shoes were getting dirtier, along with his pants day after day. He thought to himself that he was a small rock in a large current, and he needed to survive. He knew he couldn't block or change the system because he was just a child. He was going to try to live his life without making any additional waves.

The second part of eleventh grade started getting more difficult. It was difficult for Cristian to try to be receptive and not make any more waves when the history teacher was rewriting history and teaching it to his classmates. History is history. It can't be changed; however, this teacher was trying to change it. He tried to tell the class that in the 1800s, the Romanian people knew a change was coming, and it was a way to make everyone equal (communism was coming?). Cristian knew communism was not a way to make people equal. The teacher told the students it was prophesized and realized. He could not believe how many students believe this to be true—believed in the system and thought it worked. So as he told me, this teacher made his life a living hell. I only imagine Cristian had a difficult time drinking the Kool-Aid and possibly was antagonistic.

He was also listening to more news on the illegal radio stations about different manifestations taking place in different cities in Romania. Some citizens were trying to revolt against communism because there was no food, no heat, and the living conditions were intolerable. Of course, as he told this, I think listening would only fuel his passion for the hate he must have felt toward his president and the communist party and desire to leave the country. He was sixteen years old when his turn came to stand in line to buy milk beginning at ten o'clock at night. He could only wait until 7:00 a.m. because he needed to be in school by 8:00 a.m., so there were times when he would come home without milk. The store would get only ten crates, so there was not enough for all who waited. In the spring, summer, and fall, the conditions were not bad to wait, but in the winter, with the wind blowing, it was harsh to stand in that line. There were times he would stand there and piss himself because if he left the line, he would have to go all the way to the back of the line. He learned to quit eating and drinking anything before he got in line to avoid needing to use the bathroom. There were times he was successful in buying milk, and the family would really try to make it stretch, and then there were other times when he came home with none. The line to receive the maximum of three rolls of toilet paper was the same situation, and often times he wouldn't bring it home. His grandpa suggested they use newspaper, a communist newspaper, so Cristian was very proud to say he wiped his ass with communism propaganda. He was also tasked with going to the market for his grandma, and she would give him enough money for both groceries and a phone call back to her to advise her what food was available for purchase so she could choose. He remembered going to the meat market, and there were two men in butcher uniforms smoking cigarettes, listening to a small radio on the shelf, and doing nothing else because there was no meat in the store—nothing. He thought what a waste to pay two people to work and not making any profit. Basically, these were treasure hunts, not grocery shopping as we know it, and oftentimes, as he was sent out to buy groceries, he would come home with nothing.

News traveled fast that there was a government-owned company in Timisoara, Romania, close to the border of Hungary, processing meat. There was a huge pig farm, and all that was produced there was being exported and sold. The president was proud of this farm. People were traveling up to fifteen hours by train to get some food, some meat. If they were lucky enough to buy some meat, they had to worry about the police confiscating it on their way home. Not only the meat and food being produced in Romania were sold to other countries, but also the clothes, shoes, cars, and equipment that were being produced here as well. Everything that was being made in Romania was being sold to other countries, including the United States, to make payments on those defaulted loans, leaving citizens of Romania with only third-grade leftovers. This was when Cristian realized President Ceausescu was trying to brainwash the citizens of Romania, especially the school-age children, into hating America. He remembered the lessons in school of learning about the United States government and citizens were full of hatred for Romanian people.

The teachers would advise the students that the American "imperialism" was going to fail. They taught these students that the leaders of the United States hated Romania and wanted to destroy them. This was when I heard a passion and admiration in Cristian's voice as he described what he knew about the United States. He said he knew the United States was not imperialistic and that the United States was a democracy. He knew the United States was not trying to destroy Romania. He idolized the United States for its economy, military, and democracy—how citizens were able to work five days and have what is called a weekend, how they could be free to travel. He spoke so highly of what he knew about America, and I remembered thinking to myself how I had taken all this for granted—weekends, traveling, democracy. His president wanted the children to hate the United States for reasons that he knew were not true. He knew the United States, in its democracy, embraced the individual while the communist regime embraced the whole and destroyed the individual. The hatred was fed to the Romanian people every day on television, in the newspaper, in schools, and by other citizens who believed in the communist system. It was such a contradiction to reality. Romania became the weakest and poorest country in all Europe at some point because of how the communist regime was implementing the rules and manipulating people.

Cristian's grandpa never spoke a lot about his visit to the United States. Cristian figured his grandpa didn't want to stir the animosity toward Romania or stir the fuel in the fire Cristian had about being lied to about how socialism was better than democracy. Once in high school, Cristian did remember his grandpa telling him a story about being in a New York hotel. His grandfather remembered a colleague eating a doughnut right before bed. His grandpa asked the colleague where he got a doughnut, and the man told him it was from the lobby and didn't cost anything. The grandpa told the man he better go put it back because nothing was free. The man told him not only was the doughnut free, but there was also juice on the table in the lobby that was free. His grandpa woke up a colleague, who spoke English, and walked him down to the lobby to ask the receptionist about this free food. The receptionist told the men that this was free for anyone who stayed at the hotel. The following day, they stayed at a different hotel. This time, there was a buffet. Cristian's grandpa asked the same English-speaking colleague to inquire about the buffet, and again, it was free to anyone who stayed there. The men didn't know how this was possible. There was so much free food and drinks, and it was everywhere they went. Grandpa also told Cristian that he was amazed at how large the highways and buildings were. The width of the road was much wider in the United States than the road in Europe.

He remembered President Ceausescu stating he was going to construct the largest building in Romania called "The People's House." It would be the second-largest building in the entire world. As soon as he heard the president say this, Cristian could not understand how a president of a country would want to spend money to construct this building that would cost so much money to create and then need to pay for heat and electricity when the citizens did not have enough food, electric, or hot water. Romania had the farming potential to feed 80 million people and only had 20 million people. So the potential was there to feed four times the population, yet they were starving. There were stories at that time about people dying in their own apartments in the winter because they were so cold, and there was no heat. President Ceausescu did indeed hire a team of seven hundred architects to construct the heaviest building on Earth in Bucharest, almost 4,000,000 square feet, and took thirteen years to build. The value of this building was over $3 billion and cost over $6 million a year for electricity and heat, even though 70 percent of this monstrosity remained empty. You can imagine the bitterness Cristian felt in knowing the man who created so much poverty for his citizens would have something of this magnitude created for his own ego and pleasure.

In 1987, President Reagan made the infamous speech to the Soviet leader, "Mr. Gorbachev tear down this wall." Although most of us thought that was a request to tear down a physical wall dividing East Germany and West Germany, the people of Romania thought it had a deeper meaning to end communism altogether and free the people. Cristian heard the infamous speech on Voice of America and Free Europe radio and knew something was coming out of it. He didn't know what was coming, but he knew something was going to happen.

In 1987, things were very, very bad for Cristian at the age of seventeen. At the beginning of every school year, the students were put on buses and taken to the fields to work the crops because no one could trust the adults to work in fear they would steal, and the children did this as free labor. The people who were in charge of the fields would steal from the government in those fields to fill their own bellies and own pockets. These children were free labor. The children ranged from fourth graders to college students. They harvested things like corn and potatoes, whatever was in season at that time of the year. Cristian remembered 1987 being especially hard in the fall because anyone who had a garden kept and preserved their own harvest, and the stores had little to no food because they were preparing for what was told was going to be a bad winter, and it truly was a bad winter. He remembered going to the market to try to get some potatoes with a little money in his pocket because he hadn't had one in months. When he arrived at the market, the only potatoes for sale were rotten and blackened. He thought to himself that when he got to the fields the following day, he is going to take a couple of the potatoes. He was free labor, and he couldn't find potatoes at the market, so he justified taking a couple of large potatoes and putting them in his pocket. The kid just wanted some mashed potatoes or french fries. Of course, someone saw him do this and told the communist party member in charge. He was asked to empty his pockets and caught. He was told never to do that again, or he would be in trouble. It was a disappointment to wake up in the morning hungry, go to bed hungry, not be able to buy food yet harvest for free in the fields where food was being grown. This only added to his desire to leave.

During this time, there was a black market for hard-to-get items. Cristian was resourceful and inquisitive, so he knew who and what to ask to understand this process. He became a "small businessman" in the black market to get the things he needed. He found out that there were Yugoslavian tourists that would come to Romania and sell cigarettes, blue jeans, and other things and that these items could be resold for profit. He devised a plan. Saturday morning in his school was physical education, and the teacher was a former colleague of Cristian's mom. This gave him the opportunity to avoid going to school on Saturday with no retaliation. He only needed to show up three times that year and passed the class with an A+. He started his business with just two cartons of cigarettes and sold them to other students at school. Word spread very quickly, and he sold his first two cartons in just two days between classes. He made money and learned what private enterprise truly is. The following weekend, he went back and bought three cartons, the following week four. After a while, he started selling cigarettes at a five-star restaurant in the city center. Felix was the man in charge there and decided who was able to sell at this restaurant. Cristian never spoke to Felix about why he allowed him to sell cigarettes there but felt like Felix respected him for showing up at the young age of seventeen and also his ability to "keep his mouth shut." Felix gave him the trust from the beginning and told Cristian not to screw up. Cristian would sell Yugoslavian cigarettes, Niko, and BT cigarettes made in Bulgaria to members of the communist party and leaders. For him, to be able to sell cigarettes to these people as a kid was a lot. Felix must have thought, "Wow, this kid has balls. He's just a simple kid. Not a mouthy kid. Just a kid who keeps his mouth shut. Doesn't see anything. Doesn't know anything. He just brings his cigarettes and does not pretend to be something he is not." At one point, Felix even allowed Cristian to go inside and have a meal. He was excited to eat and drink in this five-star restaurant at the age of seventeen. Of course, it was before normal dining hours, but he was treated to a whiskey and a nice meal. At seventeen, this would have never been possible for him without having a connection. It was great to experience what it's like to be a party member and live like a party member without the title.

He sold Sharpie markers and chewing gum, but cigarettes were the main source of income. He did this through the rest of eleventh grade and his senior year. Business was good this year. He knew there was a risk and felt like he was given a pass from the police with this. It was stealing from the communist party, and he felt like he was somewhat protected while doing this but didn't know why. Cristian felt like the police let him alone with his enterprise because he wasn't hurting anyone or doing anything else wrong. He went to other restaurants to try to sell cigarettes, and these were just regular restaurants with regular people, so he could not charge as much. Food was scarce, so regular restaurants, functioning restaurants were more like bars. One restaurant named Transylvania was close to where he bought the cigarettes in Sarmis but far away from the five-star restaurant in Lido. There were two guys in charge who immediately told him to go back to Lido and do his business. This shook Cristian because that meant they knew who he was and what he was doing, and he had no idea how they knew that. He then realized he needed to stop. What if he got busted? A voice in his head told him he was going to be all right.

With some of his profit, Cristian also wanted to have some American dollars, actual paper bills for himself. People in Romania wanted American money because it was good trading power. You could bribe a doctor or a merchant for food, cigarettes, jeans, or shoes. Dollars were the highest bribing power someone could have. He told me obtaining American dollars was very difficult. People who sold these bills only did this a couple of times a year and hung very low in between. Getting American currency was complicated for them, and if caught, it was punishable by jail, and the police would confiscate their houses. One man was imprisoned for ten years for getting caught with a twenty-dollar bill. Cristian was able to eventually buy a one-dollar bill and a twenty-dollar bill. He didn't remember what the exchange rate was but remembered it was very, very high. Owning a twenty-dollar bill could open almost any door. He wanted to have them in his pocket for security. Selling cigarettes was risky, and he quit doing it when he graduated high school because it was really like a house of cards. Any one of those communist party members, or even Felix, could have turned on him, called the cops, and everything would have been gone in no time. He really couldn't trust anyone. He sold the last two packs of Kent cigarettes made in the United States at the restaurant and was done in the summer of 1988.

Twelfth grade was another rough year. His teachers didn't make anything easy on him and wanted him to fail. Cristian believed again that it was that chemistry teacher who was a communist party member and knew he did not pledge to the Young Communist Organization. She would make each school year going forward difficult by influencing his teachers to make him suffer. In high school, he had twelve projects due in order to graduate. The project presentations were scheduled by the staff, and he remembered when he looked at the scheduled presentation times, it was physically impossible to be present for all twelve of them. Cristian got very creative with a couple of the presentations by going, introducing himself, giving the project name, and leaving the actual paperwork for them to read later, citing that he needed to leave to get to the next presentation. He passed twelfth grade and was relieved he graduated high school. Going to college was not an option, so Cristian decided to get a job as a mechanic. This job would only pay a fraction of what he made selling cigarettes, but there was no risk.

By the time Cristian graduated high school in Romania, in the United States, the Internet was up and running in most households, and the first well-known computer virus was created. We were ending the Ronald Reagan years, and George W. Bush was elected. We witnessed music history with Live Aid and "We Are the World" in 1985. We were on opposite sides of the fence with something as trivial as "New Coke." Nintendo came out and rocked our worlds. Michael Jordan had his rookie year. Martin Luther King Day was observed for the first time. We were introduced to Prozac. There was disposable money in America. Hell, I already started a business and got myself pregnant. All this while this man was suffering in a communist country led by a psychopath leader starving its citizens and leading his country to ruin.

CHAPTER 4

A Change is Coming

After graduating high school, Cristian met his biological father for the first time on January 12, 1989. No rhyme or reason why the man reached out to Cristian. He had spoken to him on the phone a few times prior to the meeting and only remembered these conversations bitterly and for very good reasons. Cristian's dad promised him a bicycle and never bought him one. He skipped out on all child support. He gave Cristian his phone number and told him he could call anytime he wanted. Cristian told me he called his father a few times, and after maybe the fourth time, his father asked not to call him anymore. Cristian was very disappointed and confused as to why his father shut off all communication so quickly. He wondered if it was also because his father found out that he did not pledge to the Young Communist Organization but truly never really learned the reason.

Cristian was obligated to join the Romanian Army after high school in the fall of 1988 but was allowed to defer for six months. He enlisted in January 1989. He told me that the army captain was the man in charge and was also a communist party member. The captain was especially tough on Cristian, knowing he was not actively seeking to be in the communist regime. After Cristian had been in the service, just a few months, the man would beat him and throw him to the ground. Cristian could not retaliate because he would surely be thrown in prison. The man repeatedly tried to convince Cristian to become a communist member, and Cristian repeatedly refused.

Sometime after these episodes, the leader sent the sergeant major to get Cristian and bring him to the army captain's office. Once there, the man explained he would not beat him again and that they needed to talk. He told Cristian that he now realized who his grandpa was and worked to verify the mining industry. He needed help locating his little brother, who was sent to a coal mine and required to work underground for at least five years. The captain wanted Cristian's grandpa to change the assignment to something where he could work above ground. Cristian again saw the hypocrisy of this communist who needed help in reassigning a relative impacted by the same party he supported but decided to enlist the help of his grandpa. The captain went to see Cristian's grandpa and explained the situation. After he left, Cristian's grandpa called him and told him the captain had a cocky attitude but told him that if he could help, the army captain could find a way to get Cristian back home more often. Cristian told his grandfather not to accept that deal and that he would be fine. The grandfather then asked Cristian if he wanted him to assist the captain. Cristian told him not to help. The man was a hypocrite, part of the lies and manipulation, and to let the communist party help him find his brother's problem. Cristian had no idea how the story ended or if the captain ever changed his brothers' assignment, nor did he care.

In December of 1989, a violent civil unrest began in Timisoara, Romania, and quickly spread throughout socialist Romania. Romanians sought revolution and a change in government after years of social and economic depression. On December 21, President Ceausescu attempted to give a speech to eighty thousand citizens and did not realize almost all of them had turned against him. As the president started to talk about the achievements of the socialist regime, the crowd started to boo and jeer at him. The police, who had previously backed the president, had also now turned on him and supported the protesters. Cristian heard the news as it was broadcast across the country. Just four days later, on Christmas Day of 1989,

President Ceausescu and his wife stood trial, charged with genocide, damage to the national economy, and abuse of power. At the trial, one of the questions the communist president asked was why he had an account in Switzerland with $3 billion. He had replied this was not his money. They were convicted and executed the same day. They were the last executed until the death penalty was abolished the following year. The National Salvation Front immediately took power and promised fair elections and installed a series of political and democratic reforms. Although the end of socialist Romania was realized, the memory of those years could never be erased. After the execution, Cristian reflected back.

In January 1990, the Romanian government stopped exporting all food and again began to stock its own country. When Cristian came home from the army, his brother, now ten years old, had received his very first banana. His brother looked at it and sniffed it and didn't know how to eat it. He licked the outside and tried to bite that peel. The child needed to be shown how to peel and eat the banana. Cristian remembered bananas before the 1977 food shortage and how the Chiquita sticker would be removed from the peel and stuck to the wall to display the fact that a resident once had a banana to eat. Cristian got to witness his brother taking his first bite of a banana and watching his eyes open wide, enjoying the taste of the delicious fruit. He thought back to a time when he would shop for his grandma during the food shortage and have to show his identification card as well as a card that told the ration of food he was allowed to purchase. He remembered going to the bread store where he was allowed only one fourth of a ten-inch round loaf of bread, which equated to just a few slices. He remembered the government reducing the allowed calorie intake to 1,200 then down to 800 calories a day. That was the directive of the president to every living soul in Romania. Every year they had to hustle around and find someone who sold hogs and buy one for Christmas, but they had to be careful how to get it home. If the police found the hog, they would confiscate the hog, and the citizen would be in trouble. The happiest time of those years is when they would successfully get a hog home and have meat for the next few months. Now that there was a banana in the house, he thought there is a light at the end of the tunnel. There would be food for all to eat and heat in the winter. We all talked about our childhood more than we talked about our later years in life. Cristian remembered the millions of other people who suffered with him, walking down the street and seeing the grim faces of the people walking by, the millions of children like him that would have these same memories growing up, how they were not allowed to talk about the conditions they lived in.

After the execution, Cristian thought back to the early years of his life. He recalled a Sunday when his grandma seemed to have had more than she could take and said, "This is worse than the war," and his grandpa turning to look in her direction but not at her, as though their eyes met in the carpet. He knew then that if the conditions were worse than war, he needed to get out of that country. He wondered why no one could help the small country of Romania and just bring back the basics of food, eclectic, and hot water. He was always dreaming with his eyes open about living in the United States and the admiration he had for that country. He wanted to live as a free man whose rights are protected by the constitution, a constitution that was so vast and so deeply constructed to ensure the individual's rights are protected. He remembered listening to the United States sponsored radio station Free Europe one gray and gloomy Sunday, and on this segment, a woman in Florida was describing the normal life with the beach and palm trees, people walking around eating hot dogs and hamburgers, and they were all free. Freedom was the strongest statement. He pictured himself there, eating what was called a hamburger, and whatever it was, it sounded great—living in a country where you could travel without being questioned. Anyone could open a business. You could buy and sell stock. It was a country with private enterprise, a country protected by the law and the constitution. The stores were always open, and you could buy food whenever you want—the American dream.

Years after his grandpa returned from the United States, the conditions in Romania had gotten much worse. It was a cloudy, rainy day, and Cristian asked his grandpa how it was in the United States. His grandpa answered that there was no other place like the United States. The social, economic, political, and military aspects were all like no other country he had ever visited. Cristian asked if there was enough food for everyone, and his grandpa told him food was everywhere, and no one would go hungry. He added that people worked five days a week and could go anywhere they wanted on their weekends. He told Cristian that on the weekends, they go skiing or to the beach and come back Sunday evening and go back to work on Monday.

He recalled listening to By Request on illegal radio and hearing Bob Seger's "Take Down, Shake Down" for the first time when a picture of President Ceausescu picture was on the television, and the moment felt like a prophecy that someone would take down, shake down this president, and there would be freedom. Cristian still loved that song because it's something that marked him. He always listed to Casey Casem and all the 1980s music and was amazed and touched by this music. He listened to Dolly Parton and Kenny Roger's song and wondered how his president banned that music from Romania under the hatred for what he called American imperialisms.

Cristian recited the part of the pledge of allegiance that stated, "One nation, indivisible, under God," and told me he wanted to live in a country that believes in God, a nation that doesn't shut God down and knows He's in control, a country that protects the rights of its individuals. By now, Cristian's voice was very passionate, and he went on to further condemn his own president again and stated the reason his president was executed on Christmas Day of 1989 was for all the crap they did against humanity to the Romanian people, to allow children to do homework by candlelight and have your vision impaired for two or three days, not having heat in the house, not having food. These are basic human rights a child needs to develop into a normal adult who loves life and does something to prosper in life. Do something good. He never understood how this man called himself the most lovable president, the father of all children, and the genius of the Carpathian part of Europe. The reality of this president was totally different.

All this fire was building up inside of him, and he knew he had to leave Romania and get to the United States somehow. He didn't know how that would happen. On December 25, 1989, when the president was executed, Cristian was still in the military and was transferred to the same city where they got executed. He was stationed less than a mile from where the execution occurred and remembered a huge boulder being lifted off his shoulder. Cristian knew the country would see heat, see food, and also have some freedom. This was difficult for people who did not know what freedom was.

As he traveled through Europe, he still saw signs of communism in certain cities in Europe. As the years progressed, they started taking them down, but communism was a very deep-embedded system in many places in Europe. People in Eastern Europe really hated communism, the lack of transparency in this system, and the rules put on the masses. When the revolution started and the countries collapsed politically, many people thought there would be a positive way of regaining freedom and a change in the economy, but that all took a lot of time. It was very hard to rebuild and destroy what was not good and replace it with something that was good. Western Europe was being flooded by immigrants and being sent back home. It was difficult to make a decent income. Cristian knew he needed to get out, get a visa and a work permit to get to the United States legally.

After the execution in 1989, the borders opened, and Cristian was free to travel to France, Germany, Hungary and saw freedom, normal people who are not concerned with the government being part of their lives. They traveled and wore what they wanted. No one told them to turn off lights at ten o'clock at night to conserve energy. Cristian needed to see freedom in other countries and learn how people lived, but the dream still boiled inside him to live in the United States. Although there were many free countries in Europe to live in, history over the past 250 years showed countries changing and borders changing. The wars in Transnistria and Yugoslavia had changed borders and were very close to Romania. In the United States, the southern border is Mexico, the northern border is Canada, and both sides were an ocean. Those borders had not and will not change. The United States was the safest places place in the world. The fact that the United States has the only military superpower in the world. He needed to have peace and security, knowing a government would protect him. The constitution would protect him as an individual. He needed to have peace and security, knowing he was protected as an individual. His dream was to move to the United States and start a family. He needed a plan.

It was very hard to maintain a good job during the communist era. Cristian had been working as a mechanic on heavy equipment, trucks, trailers, dump trucks, etc. but did not have enough saved to pay for an expensive plane ticket. There was not enough water to clean the trucks to work on them. There would be inches of dirt accumulated on the nuts and bolts under the trucks that would need to be cleaned off before he could even start the maintenance. The money Cristian made would often go to his grandparents because he was living with them. In January 1989, he went into the Army, and the money he was paid in the Army was not even enough to buy a pack of cigarettes every day. When he got out of the Army in April of 1990, he went b ': to work as a mechanic. Inflation started to take place in Romania at that time, so it was difficult to make a living. He decided to go to work for a private contractor, doing work to guard different institutions. Military experience was required. Salary was double what he made as a mechanic. The owner of the company he worked for was arrested and taken to jail, so Cristian left Romania and went to Hungary. It was well more advanced than Romania in 1990. He went there with three friends in an attempt to sell items in Hungary that cost less in Romania. That didn't work out too well. He wanted to try Poland, Germany, and France—anything he could do to make money. He tried again in 1993 in Poland but never was successful. He couldn't find the main supplier, and customs was very tricky. During this time, he found out that his biological father was very big into the black market. He was into selling many items such as contraceptives, leather gloves, fur coats, and many other things but was very well protected. His father made a lot of money in the black market, traveling to Poland, Hungary, and Czechoslovakia.

Cristian found a way to get to the United States by applying for a job on a cruise ship. The cruise ship would dock off the coast of Florida, and although he would live on the ship, he could see the United States when it was docked. In order to apply for this job, he needed to learn the English language. He only knew ten English words, and half of them were curse words. To learn English, he decided he would watch cartoons five or six hours a day. He watched cartoons to learn the basic words in English, but he also received the subtitles in Romanian at the bottom of the screen so he could hear the English words and see the Romanian meaning. He watched daily for a couple of months and taught his self the basics of the English language prior to going on the interview. Of course, his grandmother thought he lost his mind, a "grown-ass man" watching cartoons because she didn't know the reason he was watching. There were about 530 people who applied for the positions from all over Europe, Poland, Hungary, Bulgaria, Yugoslavia, and other Eastern European countries. The job was not on United States soil but was on a cruise ship. Of the 530 people, there were only thirty-four who passed the language test, and Cristian was one of them. After, there was a medical test, and then there were about twenty-five people who passed, and again, he was one of them. About one week before Christmas in 1996, he went to the American counsel in Bucharest and obtained a visa to work in the United States on a cruise ship. About three days before Christmas, Cristian needed to clear his mind, so he was walking on the empty streets of Deva and met one of his buddies walking back home. Cristian asked his friend what Santa Claus was bringing him, and his friend replied with a few things and then asked Cristian the same. Cristian showed the friend his passport and visa to go to the United States, and the friend told him he had received the greatest gift anyone could receive. How would he pay for the airplane ticket to get to the United States?

To buy the $1,200 plane ticket and $300 in fees from Budapest to Miami, Cristian's uncle put him in touch with a man who borrowed money from the uncle to open a business and told this man to give any profit that was due to the uncle directly to Cristian as salary. This man agreed but was not a very good businessman and did not have enough to pay Cristian what he needed. Cristian's uncle, who has lived in the United States since 1970, came to visit Romania in 1996. Cristian asked his uncle if he could help him get to the United States, and his uncle said that he would help. Cristian had another uncle who lived in Kenya who came to Romania in December 1996, so Cristian asked him for the remainder. He now had the money to buy the plane ticket to freedom, and he was going to the United States. At twenty-seven years old, he was starting his life.

CHAPTER 5

America

The Delta flight to the United States was long, with a stop in Vienna. Arrival was in Atlanta, Georgia. Cristian could not believe the size of the airport and that transit was used to go from terminal to terminal. A train to go from arrivals to departures? Next stop was Miami, as this is where the cruise line was based at the time. When they got off the plane in Miami, the cab took them to the hotel, and Cristian remembered being in awe of the cab, a large American car. There were very few American cars in Romania. It was very late driving through Miami, but he remembered lots of lights and seeing many people enjoying their selves. There were many nightclubs on the street where the hotel was. He remembered in Romania, there was a curfew, and one night, when he was at a nightclub in Romania, the police showed up and asked what kind of music they were listening to. The police told them they had to listen to ten Romania songs for one song from another country. He remembered the nightclubs ultimately closing down because no one wanted to go, and they were losing money. One night, they started to open again and attempt to play United States music. Cristian would sit outside the door and listen to United States music like Frankie Goes to Hollywood and Abba and other eighties music. Cristian always believed people should listen to what they wanted as it did not inspire hate, nor could it bring down a system. When he was in Miami, it brought back those memories of him standing outside nightclubs in Romania, sitting outside of nightclubs but in Miami. I asked if he heard "We Are the World" in 1985 in Romania. He said although illegal, they were able to listen. Romania's government called it illegal as it was an inspiration for people to revolt against the system. Cristian knew the message was fighting for world hunger but, the communist regime took it as revolting. What about Live Aid? They could not watch those concerts at all. He could not believe the communist regime thought a song could create a revolution and bring down a government.

The next morning at the hotel in Miami, Cristian walked down to the breakfast buffet. He asked how much it was, and the hotel employee told him it was free. He asked what he was allowed to eat. The employee told him to eat whatever he wanted and as much as he wanted. As he looked, he saw oranges, apples, bananas, cereal, water, coffee, tea, doughnuts, eggs, sausage, cheese, and five kinds of milk. Cristian asked why they were getting breakfast, and the employee started to get aggravated but told him when companies invite employees, they often include breakfast at hotels. First thing he saw was a maple-flavored sausage, and he thought to himself, "What's a maple-flavored sausage?" Then the eggs were coming out in huge pans, and he thought, "Wow, food!"

After breakfast, Cristian started walking through Miami. He noticed an older woman getting out of her car, and she had an iguana on a leash. He thought to himself, "That can't be right!" It looked like an alligator! Again, "Wow!" He walked into a store and saw blue jeans—Levi's, Brooklyn, and all brands! He remembered he saw a pair of Brooklyn jeans in Miami in 1997 and could not believe it because people were paying a lot of money for Brooklyn jeans in Romania, and they were very hard to come by. Then he saw sneakers—Nike, Adidas, and all kinds of sneakers—anything and everything you can imagine you can simply find and buy at a store. This amazed him.

He then decided to go to the beach. When people walked by, they would say, "Hello," or "How you doing?" and this surprised Cristian because they didn't know him. He asked one of the other employees from the cruise ship why people talked, and the man told him, "This is how people are. They are friendly. They don't care where you are from. They just want to be polite. If you don't want to answer, don't answer." He now knew this happened all over the United States, "hello," "how you doing?" "what's happening?" or "God bless." This would never happen in Europe. There were so many nationalities, and those nationalities kept to their selves. The Germans, French, Italians, pretty much all were different and not like the people in the United States. He remembered looking back from high school in Romania, looking for something to wash the dirt out of his mind. People on those streets were always looking down and keeping to themselves—no smiles, nothing to be happy about. Cristian believed the people in the United States were "normal" and lived a normal life, normal human beings who say hello to others. No one forces them. It's courtesy as humans. You don't have to answer, and no one gets offended. He was shocked the first time he heard "God bless," not because he didn't believe in God but because in Romania, this would not be heard. The United States citizens were open-minded and no restrictions about speaking about God without worrying about someone cursing you or throwing a stone at his head. He didn't know how to act each time one of these messages was spoken.

In April of 1997, the cruise ship company he worked for moved from Miami to New York. He got to walk in New York, the Big Apple, a multitude of nationalities, people who went out. The Friday traffic was incredible, and Sundays were quiet. People were everywhere. He was in awe of the buildings, the streets, and how everything was constructed. The streets were perpendicular, and Broadway crossed Manhattan. He could not believe people created the roads with common sense and a business mind. People acted totally different than he met in England, Germany, or France. He thought this must be the result of democracy, freedom, a normal life. They go to work and then also enjoy themselves and live normally. The mentality was so different. He had never met anyone like these people anywhere in the world.

In New York, they were doing the two-day cruises from Friday to Sunday just offshore to Canada and no ports. He couldn't believe residents could just take the weekend and visit Canada without a passport. He had never seen a driver's license before this and was surprised to learn all the information on one. This all seemed so simple and logical now—a little card with all the information the authorities would need to know. People worked five days, played two days, and then went wherever they wanted. As he was asking these questions to a woman on the ship, she didn't understand how Cristian didn't know, how he could be so ignorant to how people lived. She told him on the weekends, United States citizens play hard, get up and go eat until they can't eat anymore, drink until they can't drink anymore, party like there is no tomorrow, take a breather from work, go home Sunday, at dinner, go to bed, and start work on Monday all over again.

He saw the Rockefeller Center, the huge financial institutions, Twin Towers, the statues of the bull and the bear in front of the New York Stock Exchange market, and he was in awe. How does a statue of a bull and a bear depict the stock market? A man across the street from the statues explained it when he asked. He told him the bull market was when the market just takes off and bear as a declining market. Cristian believed the New York Stock Exchange controls 20 percent of the world's money. He didn't know that to be true but certainly, read it from a trusted source. So he stood in front of the bull and bear statues as not only the heart of the American economy but the world economy. He felt it was a very important place where people invest over nine hundred million shares priced all differently in just one day. All this happened right here. Amazing. He knew he had a lot to learn about America. He needed to get with the program and understand the life normal people live in the United States. He could go anywhere he wanted in the United States. He could buy a house in the United States. He could buy a house in one state and live in another. The cars! Europe had Alfa Romero, Audi, BMW, Mercedes, Fiat, all the cars Europeans drive. (He add blah blah!) Nothing compares to the American car. He laughed as he recalled his buddy telling him that everyone in the United States has a car and a phone. Cristian asked how long it would take to get a phone, and the buddy told him one day! He was amazed at how many people have more than one car and that the government does not care more about taxes! They wanted you to have more cars, more of everything. The government did not care how much you have. The mentality of the American people. One nation. Indivisible, under God.

He remembered the first time he saw a King's James Version Bible in the hotel room. He thought someone had forgotten their Bible. Someone explained they are in all hotel rooms in case you forget yours, and if you do not have one, you can take it. The hotel employee told him he could read it, or if he didn't have one, he could take that one because they have plenty. That was something that he was not used to. He was taught there was no God, don't celebrate Christmas, don't celebrate Easter. He remembered being in third grade, and the teacher asked what they did the day prior, Sunday. Cristian told her he went to church with his grandma. The teacher looked at him very oddly. The teacher then called Cristian's grandmother and told her not to take a child to church and make him believe in something that does not exist, something outside the socialist system. It was too late. Cristian believes in God. He knows God carries and guides him. In the United States, he did not have to hide his love for God. He could say he went to church without retaliation. He had never heard people talk so openly about God. He was so shocked by what a normal life looks like because he had never seen it. There were so many cultures in the United States with no division and lived normally. It amazed him to see so many people having fun on a cruise ship for two days. He was surprised when people sat at the dining tables with strangers and talked to each other like they knew each other for years. He had never seen anything like that. It impressed him. He was also grateful that people were so understanding and patient with him as he learned. After a while, he learned some passengers were much wealthier than others; however, all treated each other the same. That really surprised him. In Romania, people of different wealth statuses did not socialize together.

This would be the start of his life. He would start to enjoy life. He believed God put him in the situation to know a normal life at a very young age, necessities and people were happy than living in a country where people were decaying inside with a horrible situation. He never spoke bad about his country. Being born in the country of Romania is something he is proud of, a country rich in culture and history. The socialism and communism that occurred in his lifetime were not the faults of the country itself. Dictatorship, socialism, and communism go against the people, the little people of a country who work every day. He believed God gave him an opportunity to live through all of this and make his way to the United States—the start of his life at twenty-seven-year-old. He does not regret any of it. He would have never accomplished in Romania or any of Europe what he was able to in the United States in such a short period of time.

When Cristian got to New York in 1997, twenty years after his grandfather had been there, he called his grandparents. When his grandma answered, Cristian asked for his grandpa immediately. His grandma was upset that he didn't want to speak to her, but he was just so excited to talk to his grandpa to compare what they saw in the United States. His grandpa got on the phone and had the United States maps in his hands of places he had visited like New York, Washing, DC, Chicago, Buffalo, Phoenix. The two mapped out where Cristian was standing in New York and compared to where his grandpa stayed two decades prior. The storefront where Cristian was standing was once a shoe store in 1977 and was now a restaurant. It was so exciting for him to walk with his grandpa's and his memories.

CHAPTER 6

Living the American Dream

Working on the cruise ship gave Cristian the opportunity to talk to a lot of people in the United States, citizens who owned grocery, auto parts, magazines stores, all different people working in the private sector too like doctors, food distribution, and government employees. He realized how powerful this country was talking to so many people who worked for themselves. He remembered talking to a Black woman who owned her own salon—nails and hair. She had been on a two-day cruise, and he wanted to know how she was able to enjoy the weekend and asked if she closed her shop in order to get the time. She told Cristian that she didn't need to close her business to have the weekend off. She told him that she has a manager and people working for her. Everything was taken care of, and she could afford to take two days off to do things for herself and refresh herself. Cristian didn't understand how she could leave and not be personally involved in the business, and she told him, when you have people you can trust, you can afford it, and the shop will run very smoothly. "Things going pretty smooth" was a phrase that stuck within Cristian. Years after this, he remembered these words when he opened his own business.

He left the cruise ship in 1997 after the company he worked for sold the business, and that new company went bankrupt. He went back to Romania, but before he left in 1997, he met the woman who would later become his wife. She lived in West Virginia, a state with totally different characteristics than what he had seen in Florida and New York. She came to Romania before they were married and visited Cristian. Before she left for the trip, she told him that her friends and family told her to be careful of Dracula because he lived in Romania. They told her there were vampires and to make sure she takes garlic. They told her there was no toilet paper, and the bathrooms were outside. Cristian remembered the woman calling him about three days before she was due to arrive, asking him a series of strange questions about bathrooms and strange eating habits. He laughed as he told the story about calming her fears over all the untruths she had heard.

When she came to visit, she told him the cuisine was different, and he didn't really understand that. The food in Romania was much like that on the cruise ships. Of course, the food prepared for the cruise ship passengers was prepared by master chefs. Cristian then thought maybe opening a restaurant that served Romanian food in a big city like New York was what he wanted to do. He would need the basic Romanian food products. He did some research and found out that there were two very successful Romanian restaurants in New York. One of them had some very successful regular patrons. After additional research, he found out the restaurant business is pretty risky and kept researching for a less risky business.

Cristian wanted to own a nightclub from the time he was a child. He would stand outside of nightclubs, listening to music, and he thought it was a good way to make money and take care of people. He didn't know nightclubs were open seven days a week in certain cities in the United States. When he was in Miami, he saw so many nightclubs right next to each other and so many people going in and out. He wondered how so many clubs so close to each other could be profitable. He realized later on that this was actually a good thing because people were happy about the choices, and when people were happy, they spent money, lots of money. Cristian wanted a nightclub where people had a good time, and he also had a good time. He would make some money and then possibly invest in other things. He didn't know what other things would be but had a plan.

In January 1998, Cristian came back to the United States to live with his future wife in West Virginia. He realized the diversity of restaurants there were. They had fast food, pizza shops, fine dining, and small diners. This was very different than Europe. The food was not expensive, and he could not see a lot of profit to be made. This confirmed his plan to find a location for a nightclub. He remembered going out to a bar/restaurant in the town of Elkins, and he was impressed with the number of patrons during the weekend. It was a good location on the main artery, but he felt the business was lacking something. It seemed like they needed to bring some fresh air to the town. People would travel from out of town to visit, and he thought it would be great to tap into that market.

By May of 1999, Cristian had gotten married and had a daughter. Together, they were working, taking care of the house, and taking care of their daughter. They would go away to the beach or to visit her brother in Ohio, and Cristian was trying to figure out how the business can develop, become a reality. He thought about opening a nightclub in Ohio, but his wife did not want to relocate there. She did not want to leave the remaining family. She also thought owning a business was too much work. He didn't let the idea die.

In 2004, Cristian and his wife were divorced, and he purchased his first house in America. He was surprised by how easy it was to purchase a home. All he needed was good credit and an down payment, then you were able to buy a house, very different from where he grew up. In Romania and all Eastern Europe, it was very difficult to buy a house. Right away, he thought about buying a second house, either to rent it out or to flip it to make money. He was surprised how many people owned multiple properties to rent and make money. Cristian learned it could even be more lucrative to own an apartment building with several units. He could do this in tandem with opening a nightclub. He had been working as a bartender and knew how much people like mixed drinks in West Virginia and other cities. He learned to make drinks as fast as he could and as best as he could. After two years of working as a bartender, he decided he was going to open his own.

The opportunity came in the summer of 2006. Cristian signed a rent-to-own contract for a bar with four apartments above. He thought this was a very good opportunity to make money with both the nightclub revenue and also the rent income. The building needed a lot of work, remodeling, bringing the building up to code. The place needed a different look, a different air. He remembered working very hard for the next four months, missing the opportunity to be open for the Forrest Festival, a huge event in this town that would draw in a lot of people. The people who came were not just locals but also out of state and even people from Canada. He thought, "What a great opportunity for business and the economy in the area." He opened the nightclub in October 2006. Many people were very curious to see what had changed with the opening, the music, the drinks, the atmosphere. When they came to visit the nightclub, they were very pleased, and word spread fast to other cities. Cristian had a constant flow of steady customers and new customers, and the business was really growing.

In 2008, when the market took a nosedive, he carefully watched what this did to his business and other businesses in the area. He had the opportunity to purchase another property with a diner downstairs and three apartments upstairs. This would expand his business and invest in something slightly different. After the bar would close in the wee hours of Saturday and Sunday morning, he remembered taking the customers to the diner to have breakfast, either dine in or to go. That worked out really good for him. Now he had the bar, the diner, and several rental properties. He wondered what else he could do. The sky was the limit. There was no limit. A person could own as many businesses as they wanted as long as he is capable of finding and maintaining good employees to take care of these businesses on his behalf. At some point, Cristian realized there were only twenty-four hours in a day, and he needed time to enjoy life outside of running these businesses. He stated that it was a reward a person must give themselves, especially when you own several businesses.

He realized he was not spending as much time with his daughter as he wanted to. He decided he would allow someone to rent the diner, and this allowed him to buy an apartment with three more income rentals. This allowed him to take two or three days off to charge his batteries and be away from the business. It was a feeling of relief, a feeling he didn't have before. He could disconnect from the business and enjoy his self. He took a series of mini vacations, and it felt very rewarding. It was nice to take time off and have money in his pocket to go places. It was even nice just to stay home. He was the boss, so he didn't need to have vacation approved. He earned United States dollars now and ever since he came to America. This was all so very rewarding to be able to say this dollar that he is earning has been around for quite some time and dominates the economic world. That's a feeling of accomplishment to Cristian. He told me this has a deep meaning for him, and he said it with such pride.

After a while, he bought another property outside town and lived in it. It was quiet but way too quiet for him. He wanted to live in the city of Elkins, so he moved to one of his apartments on one of the main streets until it was time to buy his own house. Right before his birthday that year, one of his buddies called him early one morning to meet and talk. They met at a restaurant and had breakfast, and the buddy asked him to take a drive. They took a short drive around the corner, and the buddy showed Cristian a beautiful old house with so much potential. The man had wanted to sell the house, and Cristian saw the beauty and potential right away. From having rental properties, he knew a lot about renovating. Cristian bought the property and signed the papers on February 24, 2013, his birthday. He went immediately and picked up his daughter to show her the house. His daughter loved the house and was impressed with how large it was. Cristian was happy because after he purchased it, the zoning changed, and with the hospital and new businesses, he had instant equity as the value of the house increased immensely. He would have available equity if he needed to borrow against it but also a large investment after he paid it off. He attributed the blessing to God. He stated that God really blessed him with this house.

Cristian told me that when you have your own business, you have to focus on today, tomorrow, the week after, the month after, and look at goals for retirement. He wanted to retire by the time he was forty-seven. He was looking at two other nightclubs in West Virginia but realized he did not have the capacity or the cash to do what he really wanted to do. The nightclub that he did have was the third largest in West Virginia for such a small area. He didn't want to move from the area because this was the city that started it all for him. He was trying to find people to work for him that were as committed to developing the business and realized people just wanted to do their nine-to-five job and not develop further.

He looked for another business in the area, but on February 11, 2017, he had a heart attack. That was a major game changer for him. He told me it was like God was telling him that he wanted to retire, and God wanted to show him what it was like to do nothing. After four months of recovery, Cristian started feeling very depressed. He couldn't do the same activities as he did prior to the heart attack, no more partying. The doctor told him that he needed to close the nightclub, or he would probably suffer more health consequences. Cristian reminded his self that this is not giving up on a dream—that he ran a successful nightclub for twelve years and how many other people can say they created a dream come true. He came from another country and made it happen. He didn't have any regrets about closing the business. He loved to bartend and run the place, ensuring all employees were working together, selling his signature wing and wing sauces, ensuring there was enough stock, and thinking in advance all the time. It was nourishment for him. He loved what he did. It was his dream, and God gave him the opportunity to live it. While some may condemn, stating God assisted with opening a nightclub, Cristian would disagree. He stated this country believes in God, and there were so many different relationships with Him. There were Baptist, Pentecostal, Catholics, Adventist, all this diversity, and he believed God Almighty would assist in making any dreams come true. Cristian believed that as long as you know what you are doing, the United States makes it easy to own and maintain a successful business. If the private sector failed here, the economy would die here. With the hope of God here, this country would flourish day by day. He prayed to God to thank Him for assisting him with creating a dream and making it come true. God kept the fire in him burning for so many years. The flame never died. Cristian was happy to be a citizen of this country and stated it with such honor. He was still amazed by the free enterprise here and how the government was hands-off, did not influence private business. He compared this to an art object that he could look at and just see how beautiful it is. Sometimes, the light on the art object was not powerful because a cloud might be blocking the natural rays, and the object did not show its natural beauty, but many times, that light shone on that object, and it showed its beauty and power and magnificence. It showed how awesome this object really was. The object is the private sector.

"Other countries do not have what we do in the United States." For the first time in any of our discussions, Cristian said "we," as a United States citizen. I could hear the pride and passion in his voice. He told me in Romania, there was so much to file and so much paperwork to do to even consider opening a business. He remembered a United States ambassador making a recommendation to the Romanian government to decrease the bureaucracy and paperwork, and the Romanian government actually reduced it by half, which still left a great deal of paperwork but was a step forward. He wished Romania would look how easy it was in the United States. He said many European countries create difficulty in opening a business that it puts the breaks on that business before it even starts.

At fifty years old, Cristian was still looking at ways to open and run a business. After the first few weeks of forced retirement, Cristian found it very difficult to sit and home and not be productive. He admitted to God that sitting at home not doing anything just about killed him. He needed to go back to work and be productive. He was able to go back to work after four months. Cristian figured retirement would come in twenty years. He wanted to try new things. It didn't matter if he's fifty or sixty. If he is able to work, he could do it.

People told him not to open a business in this economy, but he told them, "People still need to eat and drink and go places in their cars. They still travel and buy merchandise. People buy stuff all the time. People want to buy a new house or rent a new apartment. This is a country that never stops because the dollar never stops."

He thought the dollar drags the people behind them. The dollar tells people to make more, make enough for the things they want, and work harder. All of this, you do not see in other countries. There is not the fluidity and growth like there is in the United States. Even now, through the coronavirus, the United States raised unemployment benefits, gave loans to small businesses, and sent stimulus checks to keep this economy afloat. The government has the ability and potential to give back to the people and to the economy. It's a very strategic plan in this war we are carrying on with the coronavirus. The coronavirus has so much influence on people and the economy that this would be a good time to bring something new. This economy will stabilize and probably come back better. Cristian believes this is the time to come up with something new. The opportunity is here, and he has some ideas—ideas that he told me he is not ready to share.

"Give me your tired, your poor, your huddled masses yearning to breathe free, the wretched refuse of your teeming shore. Send these, the homeless, tempest-tossed to me, I lift my lamp beside the golden door."

I cannot wait to see what comes next, Cristian.

APPENDIX FROM CRISTIAN

Socialism

A lot of people in this country and other places around the world are wanting to have socialism—free socialism, free stuff in socialism. Got some news for you, there is no free anything with socialism—no free health care, no free housing, no freedom. Nothing is free with socialism. Socialism is a different form of communism. When you talk about redistribution of wealth, that's how communism evolved all over this world, destroying, conquering, manipulating, and devastating everything that was prosperous.

Romania between the two World Wars was the bread and basket of Europe. At the end of 1989, Romania was probably the second poorest country in Europe. All this thanks to a socialist-communist regime that destroyed everything. I never talk about my feelings during socialism. Not just me but millions of people were lied to, manipulated, brainwashed, indoctrinated, kept in hunger and cold. These people were angry because they realized there were other places around this world where people lived a decent life, under decent conditions with the basics of life. They had food, shelter, and heat without being brainwashed. I asked myself many times how come other countries have and we don't have.

Socialism is about destroying people, lying to people, keeping people hungry in the dark and in the cold. We do not want that. For those of you who want socialism, it is not a solution. People want to be free. People do not want to be controlled by a government that will tell you how much to eat, how much you have to work to meet your quota, and anything and everything about controlling people. This is not how a government should make sure people are living a good life. Socialism did all of that, and we need to rethink what we want in this life and what we want for this country. Socialism would be very bad for not only this country but also for the entire world. If the United States fails as a democratic and free-spirited country that protects the individual, it's going to collapse the entire world.

I will not apologize to anyone for speaking against socialism because I lived a part of my life in inhumane conditions. There is nothing good associated with socialism. A lot of people around the world say socialism is an alternative to have more goods or free health care, but this is not possible. We will have to work three times as hard to achieve this. The income will not be the same because socialism speaks to everyone being the same. In practice, this is not possible— in theory, yes, in practice, no.

With all said, I hope that there is something to be learned in all of this. Some people call it an experiment in some countries. Millions of people went through this experiment, and it went very, very bad for too long. As I think about socialism, it's a very dark and hard to live place that I went through, and I'm glad it's over in Romania and other countries around the world. Freedom of choice and freedom of people came in place, along with a private economy and good welfare for millions of people.

ABOUT THE AUTHOR

Linda Martin graduated high school in 1982 and went right to the school of hard knocks. College was not a priority. She was married immediately after high school and had her first child within two years. Owning and operating several businesses like pressure washing, carpet cleaning, restaurant, and grass cutting, in tandem with waiting tables and working for a financial institution, she had little time to read books, let alone think back to the times she loved writing stories as a young girl.

She grew up in the Northeast and stayed married for thirty-six years. After filing for divorce in 2018, she moved to her dream destination on the east coast of Florida. Reading at the beach every weekend, and reconnecting with so many friends over the next six months inspired the thought of one day writing again. It wasn't until she heard the voice and story of an incredible Eastern European friend and his courageous passion for rejecting communism and socialism that she was truly inspired to write again.

CPSIA information can be obtained
at www.ICGtesting.com
Printed in the USA
BVHW090218261021
619846BV00020B/1186